BASEBALL

TRIVIA

By Brian Howell

SportsZone

An Imprint of Abdo Publishing
abdopublishing.com

abdopublishing.com

Published by Abdo Publishing, a division of ABDO, PO Box 398166,
Minneapolis, Minnesota 55439. Copyright © 2016 by Abdo Consulting
Group, Inc. International copyrights reserved in all countries. No part of
this book may be reproduced in any form without written permission from
the publisher. SportsZone™ is a trademark and logo of Abdo Publishing.

Printed in the United States of America, North Mankato, Minnesota
082015
012016

THIS BOOK CONTAINS
RECYCLED MATERIALS

Editor: Patrick Donnelly
Series Designer: Jake Nordby

Library of Congress Control Number: 2015945860

Cataloging-in-Publication Data
Howell, Brian.
 Baseball trivia / Brian Howell.
   p. cm. -- (Sports trivia)
 ISBN 978-1-68078-001-7 (lib. bdg.)
 Includes bibliographical references and index.
 1. Baseball--Miscellanea--Juvenile literature.   2. Sports--Miscellanea--
Juvenile literature.   I. Title.
 796.357--dc23

                                        2015945860

CONTENTS

Major League Baseball (MLB) has a long and storied history. The National League (NL) dates back to 1876. The American League (AL) began play in 1901. Along the way, fans have witnessed thousands of outstanding games featuring amazing players and teams.

But even after all those years, baseball can still amaze its fans. Every day it seems something happens that has never been seen before. This book highlights some of the greatest teams and players in MLB history. It also uncovers some of the most unique records and events in the sport's past. How well do you know baseball? Read on to find out!

*All statistics and answers are current through the 2014 MLB season.

CHAPTER 1

ROOKIE

Q **Who was the first black player in the modern era (after 1900) of the major leagues?**

A Jackie Robinson broke MLB's color barrier on April 15, 1947. The league had a few black players before 1900. But the owners gradually stopped signing them. Soon it became an unwritten rule: MLB was for whites only. That changed when Robinson joined the Brooklyn Dodgers. The 28-year-old was named the NL Rookie of the Year in 1947. Two years later, he won the NL Most Valuable Player (MVP) Award. Robinson opened the door for hundreds of black players to come after him.

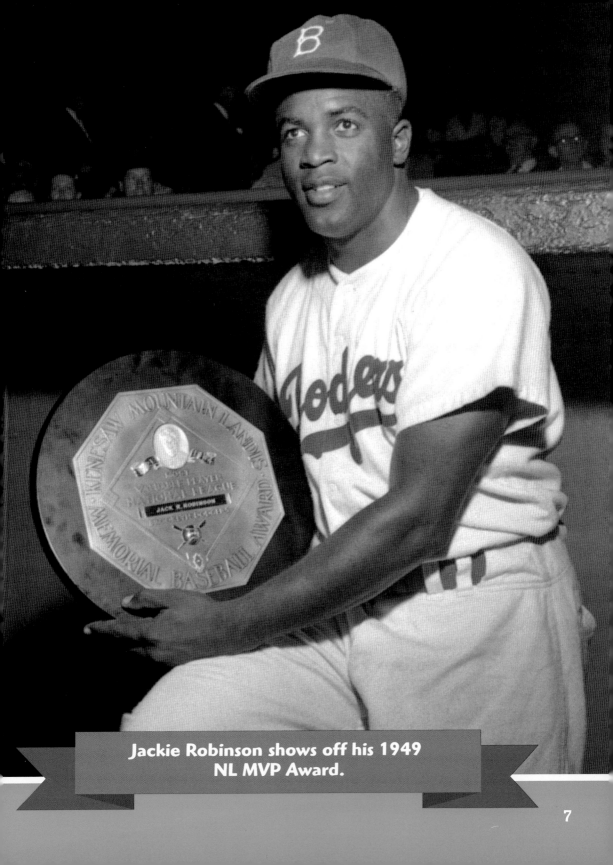

Jackie Robinson shows off his 1949
NL MVP Award.

Q Which team has won a record 27 World Series titles?

A The New York Yankees are the kings of the Fall Classic. Their 27 championships are 16 more than any other team. The Bronx Bombers have been to the World Series 40 times. They won their first in 1923. And they have won at least one title in all but one decade since then.

Q Who was the first player to earn $1 million per season?

A Pitcher Nolan Ryan was the first to hit the $1 million mark. He signed a free-agent deal with the Houston Astros in November 1979. The contract paid him $1,125,000 per season. Ryan was worth it, too. The Hall of Famer threw seven career no-hitters. He also struck out 5,714 batters. Those are both MLB records.

RYAN HAS TIED SANDY KOUFAX'
MAJOR LEAGUE RECORD OF 97
GAMES WITH 10 OR MORE
STRIKEOUTS

Q **Which two NL teams moved to their current cities from New York?**

A The Los Angeles Dodgers and the San Francisco Giants have been rivals on the West Coast since 1958. Before that they were neighbors in New York. The Giants played mostly at the Polo Grounds in Upper Manhattan. The Dodgers were 15 miles (24 km) away in Brooklyn. Both teams moved to California after the 1957 season.

Q **Which stadium has the tallest outfield wall?**

A Fenway Park in Boston features the 37-foot (11-m) Green Monster in left field. No outfield fence in the major leagues is higher. When Fenway Park was built, the neighborhood was cramped. There was not much space in left field, so the fence there sits only 310 feet (94 m) from home plate. The high wall was built to cut down on home runs to left field.

Q **Who holds the record for most consecutive games played?**

A Cal Ripken Jr. played in 2,632 consecutive games. His streak started on May 30, 1982. He broke the previous record—2,130 games, held by Lou Gehrig—on September 6, 1995. Ripken kept the streak going for three more years. He spent his entire 21-year career with the Baltimore Orioles. Ripken was a two-time AL MVP and won the AL Rookie of the Year Award in 1982.

Q Who holds the single-season and career records for home runs?

A Barry Bonds of the San Francisco Giants retired in 2007 with 762 career home runs. That broke the mark of 755 held by Hank Aaron. Bonds hit a single-season record 73 homers in 2001. The previous record was 70, set by the Cardinals' Mark McGwire just three years earlier. However, Bonds, McGwire, and many other sluggers of that era have come under suspicion. They are believed to have used performance-enhancing drugs to illegally boost their power.

Q Who won the most career Cy Young Awards?

A Roger Clemens holds that record. The Cy Young Award is given every year to the best pitcher in each league. Clemens won it seven times. No other pitcher has won it more than five times. The man known as "The Rocket" won three Cy Young Awards as a member of the Boston Red Sox. He added two more with the Toronto Blue Jays. Then he won it once with the New York Yankees and once with the Houston Astros. Clemens won 354 games and struck out 4,672 hitters from 1984 to 2007. However, like many players from his era, Clemens was suspected of using illegal performance-enhancing drugs.

Q **In 2012 Detroit Tigers star Miguel Cabrera became the first player in 45 years to accomplish what batting feat?**

A Cabrera won the Triple Crown in 2012. To win the Triple Crown, a player must lead his league in batting average, home runs, and runs batted in (RBIs). Cabrera posted a .330 batting average, 44 home runs, and 139 RBIs in 2012. He was the first player

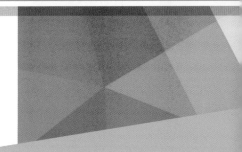

Miguel Cabrera tips his cap to the crowd in Kansas City after clinching the Triple Crown in the last game of the 2012 season.

to win the Triple Crown since Boston's Carl Yastrzemski won it in 1967.

Q **Which pitcher has the most career wins, losses, and innings pitched in MLB history?**

A From 1890 to 1911, Cy Young piled up 511 wins and 316 losses. He also threw 7,356 innings. In those days, it was common for pitchers to throw more innings and appear in more games than they do today. Because of that, most of Young's records are not likely to be broken.

HOW LONG WAS JOE DIMAGGIO'S RECORD-SETTING HITTING STREAK IN 1941?

The New York Yankees star collected a hit in 56 consecutive games. The streak began on May 15. On July 17 Di Maggio went 0-for-3 with a walk in Cleveland. Indians third baseman Ken Keltner twice robbed him of hits with great defensive plays. The next day DiMaggio started a 16-game hitting streak. No MLB hitting streak has topped 44 games since.

CHAPTER 2

VETERAN

Q Who is the only pitcher in history to win at least 15 games in 17 consecutive seasons?

A Greg Maddux was one of the most consistent pitchers in MLB history. From 1988 to 2004, Maddux won at least 15 games in every season. He spent most of his career with the Chicago Cubs and the Atlanta Braves. Maddux retired after the 2008 season with 355 career wins. He also won four consecutive NL Cy Young Awards (1992–95).

Q Which team in 2007 won 21 of 22 games before being swept in the World Series?

Greg Maddux throws a pitch for
the Chicago Cubs.

A Beginning on September 16, the Colorado Rockies won 13 of their last 14 games. That forced a one-game tiebreaker for the NL wild-card spot. The Rockies beat the San Diego Padres in that game. Then they swept the Philadelphia Phillies in three games in the NL Division Series. They also swept the Arizona Diamondbacks in four straight to win the NL Championship Series. But after winning 21 of 22 games, the Rockies ran out of gas. The Boston Red Sox swept them in the World Series.

Q How much did the New York Yankees pay to get Babe Ruth from the Boston Red Sox?

A Babe Ruth was the biggest star in baseball in 1919. However, Red Sox owner Harry Frazee had money problems. So he sold Ruth to the New York Yankees for $100,000. During the next 12 years, Ruth led the AL in home runs 10 times. He also helped the Yankees win their first four World Series titles.

Q Who is the only pitcher to throw a perfect game in the postseason?

A Don Larsen picked a good time for the best game of his life. The New York Yankees pitcher had a career record of 81–91. He never made an All-Star team. But in Game 5 of the 1956 World Series, he was perfect. Larsen retired all 27 Brooklyn Dodgers hitters he faced. Through 2014 it was one of just 23 perfect games in baseball history.

Q Which Hall of Famer holds the record for highest career batting average?

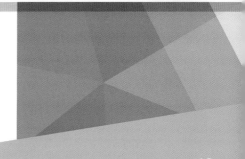

Catcher Yogi Berra, 8, leaps into Don Larsen's arms after the Yankees right-hander pitched a perfect game in the 1956 World Series.

A Nobody had more success swinging a bat than Ty Cobb. In a 24-year career that ended in 1928, Cobb posted a lifetime batting average of .366. He played 22 years with the Detroit Tigers and led the AL in hitting 12 times. Cobb still ranks second in history in hits (4,189), triples (295), and runs scored (2,244).

Q **Who was the last pitcher to win at least 25 games in a season?**

A Oakland's Bob Welch won 27 games in 1990. The league leaders once won 25 games or more on a regular basis. But that changed when most teams went to a five-man starting rotation in the 1970s. Now starting pitchers get at most 34 or 35 starts if they stay healthy the entire season. That limits their opportunity to pile up the wins.

Q **Which two AL teams went more than 85 years without a World Series title, then won it back-to-back in 2004 and 2005?**

A In 1917 the Chicago White Sox won the World Series. The following year the Boston Red Sox won the title. It would be 86 years before either team would win another title. The Red Sox finally ended their drought by sweeping the St. Louis Cardinals in the

John Smoltz was an ace starter and an All-Star closer for the Atlanta Braves.

2004 World Series. The next year, the White Sox swept the Houston Astros for their first title in 88 years.

Q **Who is the only man to play in at least 2,500 games but never appear in the playoffs?**

A Hall of Famer Ernie Banks played in 2,528 games—all with the Chicago Cubs—from 1953 to 1971. During those years, the Cubs were one of the worst teams in baseball. Also, fewer teams qualified for the postseason in that era. Through 2014 Banks was one of 55 players to have appeared in at least 2,500 games. The other 54 all played in the playoffs at least once.

Q Which NL team has the most all-time victories?

A The Giants have been playing in the major leagues since 1883. They began play as the New York Gothams. Through 2014 the Giants had 10,780 regular-season victories. And after going 55 years without a title, they won three World Series between 2010 and 2014.

WHO IS THE ONLY PITCHER IN HISTORY WITH AT LEAST 200 CAREER WINS AND 150 CAREER SAVES?

During his 21-year career, John Smoltz won 213 games and recorded 154 saves. The longtime Atlanta Braves star was a dominant starting pitcher from 1989–99. But Smoltz had elbow surgery and missed the 2000 season. When he returned in 2001, he began his comeback in the bullpen. Smoltz dominated as a closer for more than three years. He returned to the starting rotation in 2005 and won another 50 games.

CHAPTER 3

CHAMPiON

Q Which shortstop was nicknamed "The Wizard" because of his exceptional play on defense?

A Throughout his 19-year career, Ozzie Smith was known as "The Wizard." Smith played for the San Diego Padres and the St. Louis Cardinals from 1978 to 1996. He will be remembered as one of the best defensive shortstops ever. He was a 15-time All-Star and won 13 Gold Glove Awards. Every year, the Gold Glove is awarded to the best fielder at each position.

Ozzie Smith shows his stuff at the 1987
All-Star Game.

Q Which teams played in MLB's first night game and first televised game?

A On May 24, 1935, the Cincinnati Reds and Philadelphia Phillies squared off at Cincinnati's Crosley Field in the first night game. The Reds again made history four years later. On August 26, 1939, they played a doubleheader against the Brooklyn Dodgers at Ebbets Field. The games were shown on W2XBS television, making them the first televised games.

Q Who played on the most World Series championship teams?

A Yogi Berra won 10 World Series titles during his 18 seasons with the Yankees (1946–63). Amazingly, the Yankees won the AL pennant 14 times in that span. Berra was one of the greatest players and most colorful characters in baseball history. He played in 15 All-Star Games and was voted into the Baseball Hall of Fame.

Hank Aaron hit a lot of home runs but never 50 in a season.

Q **Eight players in history have hit at least 600 career home runs. Which of them never had a 50-home-run season?**

A Hank Aaron was one of the greatest home-run hitters of all time. With 755 career home runs, he was baseball's all-time leader for 33 years. But his single-season high was 47 homers in 1971.

Q Who is the only player in history to pitch consecutive no-hitters?

A Cincinnati's Johnny Vander Meer had quite a week in 1938. On June 11, the 23-year-old left-hander threw a no-hitter in a 3–0 win against the Boston Bees. Four days later, Vander Meer no-hit the Brooklyn Dodgers in a 6–0 win. Despite allowing no hits, he was not especially dominant in those two games. In 18 innings he walked 11 batters and struck out only 11.

Q Who is the only rookie to win the Cy Young Award?

A Fernando Valenzuela had an amazing 1981 season with the Los Angeles Dodgers. He started his first full year in the majors with eight straight complete-game victories. Five of them were shutouts. Los Angeles was hit with "Fernandomania." The 20-year-old Mexican won the NL Cy Young Award. He also was a shoo-in for the Rookie of the Year Award. Additionally, Valenzuela helped the Dodgers win the World Series that season.

Fernando Valenzuela was a rookie sensation for the Los Angeles Dodgers in 1981.

Q Which Hall of Famer is nicknamed "The Say Hey Kid"?

A Willie Mays is considered by some to be the greatest player of all time. The reason behind his colorful nickname is not clear. He began his career in 1951, winning the NL Rookie of the Year Award with the New York Giants. He also was a two-time MVP and a 20-time All-Star.

Q Rickey Henderson led the AL in stolen bases 11 times in 12 years (1980–91). Who interrupted his streak?

A Harold Reynolds of the Seattle Mariners led the AL with 60 steals in 1987. It was Reynolds's career-best total. It was also the only time he led the league. Injuries limited Henderson to 95 games that season. But he still stole 41 bases to finish fifth in the AL.

Q Who was the youngest player to ever appear in an MLB game?

Rickey Henderson, *bottom*, steals a base against the Toronto Blue Jays in 1985.

A On June 10, 1944, 15-year-old Joe Nuxhall pitched two-thirds of an inning for the Cincinnati Reds. That was his only appearance that season and for several more years. In 1944 most MLB teams had openings in their lineups. Many of their regular players were fighting in

World War II. When the war ended in 1945, most of the players returned to baseball action. Nuxhall resurfaced in the major leagues in 1952. This time he stuck around for 15 years and won 135 career games.

Q Who is the only player with at least 3,400 career hits but no single-season batting titles?

A Derek Jeter was a star with the New York Yankees from 1995 to 2014. His 3,465 career hits ranked him sixth all time when he retired. But he never led the AL in batting average. He was second twice and third in two other seasons.

WHO IS THE ONLY PLAYER TO HIT TWO GRAND SLAMS IN THE SAME INNING?

Fernando Tatis of the St. Louis Cardinals did it on April 23, 1999. Tatis hit both homers off Los Angeles Dodgers pitcher Chan Ho Park. The Cardinals scored 11 runs in that inning, all off Park.

CHAPTER 4

HALL OF FAMER

Q How many teams have lost the first three games of a playoff series and then gone on to win the series?

A In 2004 the Boston Red Sox became the only team in MLB history to do it. For Boston fans, it was even sweeter that it came against the rival New York Yankees. The Yankees were three outs away from a four-game sweep in the AL Championship Series (ALCS). But Boston rallied to win that game and the next three to take the series.

The Red Sox celebrate after beating the Yankees in Game 7 of the 2004 ALCS.

Q Which current NL team was formerly nicknamed the Beaneaters, Bees, Doves, and Rustlers?

A Founded in 1876, the Braves have had a lot of name and location changes. They played in Boston from 1876 to 1952. They cycled through all five of their nickname changes there. They finally settled on the Braves for good in 1941. The team moved to Milwaukee in 1953 and to Atlanta in 1966.

Q Why were eight members of the 1919 Chicago White Sox banned from baseball?

A They were accused of receiving money from gamblers to fix the 1919 World Series. That means they allegedly were paid to help the Cincinnati Reds win the Series. The eight players—including ace pitcher Eddie Cicotte and star outfielder "Shoeless" Joe Jackson—were never found guilty of the fix. However, MLB commissioner Kenesaw Mountain Landis banned them for life after the 1920 season.

Eddie Gaedel drew a four-pitch walk in his only big league plate appearance.

Q **How short was Eddie Gaedel—the shortest player in MLB history?**

A He was just 3 feet, 7 inches (1.1 m) tall. But Gaedel was not a regular player. St. Louis Browns owner Bill Veeck loved a good stunt. He tried to entertain fans and sell tickets. On August 19, 1951, Browns sent Gaedel, a 26-year-old actor, to the plate as a pinch-hitter. Detroit

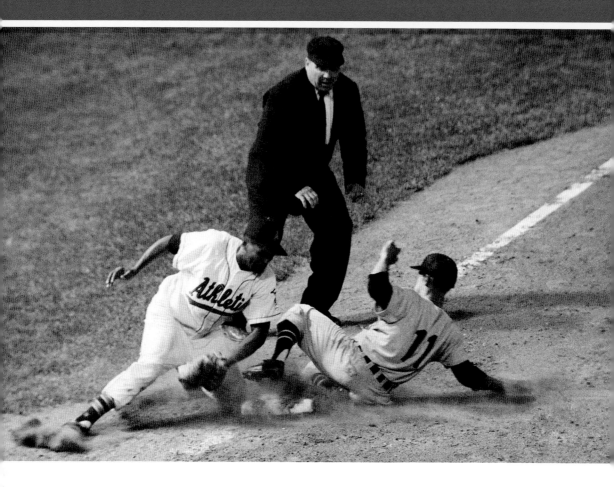

Tigers pitcher Bob Cain walked him on four pitches.
Gaedel was immediately replaced by pinch runner Jim
Delsing and never played again.

Q **Who is the only player to appear in the World Series with four different teams?**

A Lonnie Smith played for six teams in his 17-year career. He helped four of them get to the World Series. Smith won his first World Series with the Philadelphia Phillies in 1980. He won it again in 1982 with the St. Louis Cardinals and in 1985 with the Kansas City Royals. Smith made it back with the Atlanta Braves in 1991 and 1992 but lost both years.

Q One pitcher in MLB history gave up a home run to the first batter he ever faced and hit a home run in his first career at-bat. Who was it?

A Dave Eiland holds that unusual distinction. As a rookie with the New York Yankees,

WHICH PLAYER HOLDS THE RECORD FOR MOST CONSECUTIVE SEASONS LEADING HIS LEAGUE IN STEALS?

Luis Aparicio led the AL with 21 stolen bases as a rookie in 1956. But he did not stop there. Aparicio was the AL's stolen-base king for the next eight years as well. He played seven of those seasons with the Chicago White Sox. The last two titles came with the Baltimore Orioles. He stole a career-high 57 bases in 1964 to win his last stolen-base crown.

Eiland gave up a home run to the first batter he faced, Milwaukee's Paul Molitor, on August 3, 1988. Then on April 10, 1992, Eiland was playing for the San Diego Padres. He blasted a home run off the Dodgers' Bobby Ojeda in his first career at-bat. It was the only home run Eiland ever hit in the big leagues.

Q **During the 1988 World Series, how many times did NL MVP Kirk Gibson of the Los Angeles Dodgers come to the plate?**

A Just once, but it was a memorable appearance. After having an excellent regular season, Gibson injured his knee and hamstring during the playoffs. He was not supposed to play against the Oakland Athletics in the World Series. But with two outs in the bottom of the ninth inning of Game 1, the Dodgers trailed 4–3. Manager Tommy Lasorda asked Gibson to pinch hit. Gibson was barely able to walk, but he smacked a two-run homer off future Hall of Fame pitcher Dennis Eckersley. It was his only at-bat during the five World Series games. But it sparked the Dodgers to a title.

Q How long did it take to play the longest game in MLB history?

A On May 8, 1984, the Chicago White Sox and the Milwaukee Brewers began a game that lasted a record 8 hours and 6 minutes. It was suspended after 17 innings and resumed the next day. Finally, in the bottom of the 25th inning, Chicago's Harold Baines ended the game with a solo home run.

A Boston Red Sox outfielder Carroll Hardy got the call on September 20, 1960, in Baltimore. Williams fouled a pitch off his leg in the first inning and had to leave the game. It was the only time in 19 seasons that Williams was replaced by a pinch hitter. Hardy finished the at-bat by hitting into a double play.

Q How many pitchers did the Boston Braves and the Brooklyn Robins use during their 26-inning, 1-1 tie on May 1, 1920?

A Just two—Joe Oeschger and Leon Cadore. Both starters went the distance. Boston's Oeschger and Brooklyn's Cadore pitched all 26 innings, matching zeroes from the seventh inning on. The game eventually was called because of darkness at 6:50 p.m. It remains the only 26-inning game in major league history.

Q Which team holds the record for the most runs scored in a game since 1901?

A The Texas Rangers trailed the Baltimore Orioles 3–0 after three innings on August 22, 2007. During the next six innings, however, the Rangers piled up 30 runs to win 30–3. They became the first team since 1897 to score 30 runs in a game.

TRIVIA QUIZ

1 Who was the slugger nicknamed "Mr. October"?

a. Derek Jeter

c. Reggie Jackson

b. Babe Ruth

d. Hank Aaron

2 Which Los Angeles Dodgers star pitched a record 59 consecutive scoreless innings?

a. Orel Hershiser

c. Sandy Koufax

b. Fernando Valenzuela

d. Clayton Kershaw

3 How many years did Connie Mack manage the Philadelphia Athletics?

a. 15

c. 21

b. 50

d. 1

4 Who was the first player to win MVP and Rookie of the Year honors in the same season?

a. Fred Lynn, Red Sox, 1975

c. Derek Jeter, Yankees, 1996

b. Jose Canseco, A's, 1986

d. Rod Carew, Twins, 1967

5 Who hit a walk-off home run in Game 7 of the 1960 World Series between the Yankees and the Pirates?

a. Roberto Clemente

b. Mickey Mantle

c. Yogi Berra

d. Bill Mazeroski

6 Which St. Louis Cardinals slugger won three MVP Awards from 2005 to 2009?

a. Mark McGwire

b. Albert Pujols

c. David Freese

d. Matt Holliday

7 Who is the only pitcher to throw a no-hitter on Opening Day?

a. Bob Feller, Indians, 1940

b. Jack Morris, Tigers, 1984

c. Chris Sale, White Sox, 2013

d. Nolan Ryan, Angels, 1973

8 Who in 2014 became the youngest player to win his third Cy Young Award?

a. Felix Hernandez, Mariners

b. Cole Hamels, Phillies

c. Clayton Kershaw, Dodgers

d. Justin Verlander, Tigers

9 Which slugger has the most home runs ever by a switch hitter?

a. Eddie Murray

b. Chipper Jones

c. Mark Teixeira

d. Mickey Mantle

*Answers on page 47

GLOSSARY

banned
To not be allowed to participate in an activity.

drought
A long period without success.

no-hitter
A game in which a pitcher does not allow any hits.

perfect game
A game in which a pitcher does not allow any base runners and retires every batter he faces.

pinch hit
To bat in place of someone else.

postseason
The playoffs, including the wild-card round, divisional playoffs, league championship series, and World Series.

slugger
A player who hits a lot of home runs.

sweep
Winning every game in a series.

FOR MORE INFORMATION

Books

Bryant, Howard. *Legends: The Best Players, Games, and Teams in Baseball*. New York: Philomel Books, 2015.

Graves, Will. *The Best MLB Pitchers of All Time*. Minneapolis, MN: Abdo Publishing, 2014.

Jacobs, Greg. *The Everything Kids' Baseball Book*. Fairfield, OH: Adams Media, 2012.

Websites

To learn more about Sports Trivia, visit **booklinks.abdopublishing.com**. These links are routinely monitored and updated to provide the most current information available.

Answers

1.	c	**6.**	b
2.	a	**7.**	a
3.	b	**8.**	c
4.	a	**9.**	d
5.	d		

INDEX

About the Author

Brian Howell has been a sports journalist for more than 20 years, writing about high school, college, and professional athletics. In addition, he has written books about history. A native of Colorado, he lives in Denver with his wife and four children.